THE SUN RISES IN THE WEST

Sofia Romulan

The never ending what ifs

What if I lost my sight

Who will help me

Who will be there for me

What if

I was lost

In a never ending desert

With no where to go

Nothing to drink

I drive myself insane

With worries

The road is bleak

And lonely

Never ending

Infinite

With no light on sight

Cause I lost my ability to see

My brain is so powerful

My own worst enemy

It gives life to my own creations

They grow stronger and stronger

While I cower in the corner

Giving birth to more creatures

When they see the beauty

I see the danger hidden

I think about how it can be used

To alter their perception

How it can deceive them

A byproduct of

My poisoned mind

We lost the ability

To cherish

A fine dinner

A well made shelf

We lost the ability

To take our time

In doing things

All we search for

Is the instant gratification

The instant moment

The selfie

We stopped caring for the memories

And we immortalized the moments

We needed the physical evidence

And stopped looking for the emotional

We lost our sense of life

I am growing

Time has no mercy

I am developing

Into an older being

But on the inside

I am still young

Inexperienced

A small seed

That has lost the will

To grow

But time won't wait for me

So either I hop on its train

Or forever I'll be left

In my own time

I developed the habit

Of listening to others

Complain

Try to give them advice

But the more I listened

The more they complained

Until I couldn't take it anymore

But they continued

And continued

So I had to leave

To take a break

And then

I was accused of abandoning

Of changing

Of being a bad friend

I thought we would be together

Forever

For all eternity

Against all

We would triumph

Through mud

We will swim

From burning fires

We will emerge

Untouchable

But then reality

Hit me hard

Woke me up from my dream

The end was no where to be seen

And there I was drifting in my inner sea

Burning my last dreams

To satisfy the anger inside

Waiting for the moment

When it slept

So I can flee

I am starting to lose hope

As I am running out of my hopes

And dreams

I have no more dreams

To feed this monster

Its pitiful eyes

Looking at me

Waiting for me to act

To please

To give it space to vent

I am trying hard

To keep it at bay

Away from my body

I won't let it control me

At night

I whisper to myself

With a voice

Only I can hear

Afraid that they would laugh

If they see me

So I wait

For the silence

For it is the mark

That I am finally safe

In my loneliness

It's going to be okay

Air

The invisible invader

You penetrate my deepest parts

I wish I could live

Without you

You made me realize

How weak I am

How dependent I am

The basic ingredient of life

Do I have to rely on you

To be able to continue

Sometimes I try to get away

Step by step

But I come back running

Gasping

Regretting what I have done

They needed a listener

With a low toned voice

A voice that would agree

Clap at their words

Marvel at their wisdom

But I can't do it anymore

I know they will hate me

Ignore me

If I speak louder than they do

Maybe that is what I need

I yearn for the emptiness

The silence

The void

I want to be free

From the hordes of ideas

Invading my mind

Feasting on my sanity

Bit by bit

I can feel my reasoning

Slipping

Like water from my hands

I just wish I could save what is left

Of me

A question plagued my mind

Is this a test

Is there a reason

For all this to happen

To me

Am I really in control

Do I have a choice

Or am I just being driven

To my own demise

My driver has shut the doors

Put steel bars between me and him

I even can't see him any more

I have been here my whole life

When did I even get on to this ride

Did I choose to be here

Or am I just a passenger

Destined to watch but not interfere

Be a good little person

Accept and pretend

Not to notice

I am lost

Unsure

Insecure

I tend to forget

Pretend to not remember

Bury my memories in a grave

That I rarely visit

But it is always there

In the back of my mind

A simple breeze of air

Touching me gently behind my back

Light and Darkness

Inside me

Both creatures live

intertwined

Light and darkness

Inseparable

I started to believe

I started to see myself through their eyes

Damaged and broken

Enervated

Cry all you want

Cry until you fill cups and rivers

Cry all the poison away

Own your sadness

And despair

Acknowledge the pain

Sail through the storms

Until you are clean

Until you are free

From your own prison

Sometimes I wish I had

The strength

The power

The resolve

To help others

To be there

To be the one

Who approaches first

But then I remember

all those times

I was hurt

And I stop myself

I can see the tears dwelling in your eyes

The sadness living

Rent free

A stranger I am living

With no place to call home

Treating this space

As a temporary place

I have no attachments

No regrets

All Alone

In the desert of my heart

I search

For a glimpse of hope

For a little bit of light

To guide the way

All I see is yellow

Devoid of any life

Silently I pray

For a little bit of rain

As I run from space to space

Back and forth

Until my feet bleed

Leaving a trail

For any one who tries to follow

Surrounded

I am surrounded

All these demons

Are clawing at me

Shredding apart my sanity

My hopes

My dreams

My longing for happiness

Leaving me alone

With my angry thoughts

Separating me from my strength

My power

I wish I could run

But nowhere is free

Slowly I am losing myself

Poison

A river flows within me

Filling my insides with poison

It traverses through my be veins

Carried by my blood

Filling my heart and soul

Damping my mind

Alive

I'm alive

Against all odds

Contrary to all what they said

I survived

The taunts

The bullying

I know I'm still weak

But at least I won't crumble

I'm still here

Slowly breathing

Slowly growing

Slowly believing in myself

Grief

There is nothing there

Empty I feel

You can't project love

To a vessel

That vanished

A black hole

That can't process

The strength of any emotion

I am existing

Mechanically

With no soul

A desert void of life

Let Them Go

I know I will miss them

But I can't continue this

Anymore

I have to stop

It's sad to stop

Suddenly

But I am tired

Exhausted

At the beginning

I faltered

Walked with a heavy step

Not expecting to feel

To drown

In happiness

But then I learned the truth

Too much happiness

Can kill

Snooze

I kept on pressing

Day after day

Night after night

I stayed in my place

Snoozing it all the way

Let's give them one more chance

One more time

It won't hurt that much

You're already used to this kind

Of pain

Of negligence

A Fight

They don't understand

Sometimes it's as scary as a lion

Roaring inches from your face

As giant as a mountain

Weighing heavily on my chest

Leaving me gasping for air

Other times it's invisible

Even I forget it's there

Hiding in the shadows of my mind

I am searching for someone

To give

To make them feel

The things I am desperate to feel

As I am

Incapable of loving myself

Will I be able

To give to others

What I lack

What I can't give to myself

I woke up

To the sun shining

From the west

A sudden change

I couldn't fathom

I couldn't pretend to understand

Is this a sudden change

Or was this the truth all along

Did I chose to ignore

The signs

Or where they deliberately hidden

Behind my ignorance

My fear that I will be exposed

The undeniable truth is mocking me

Taunting me

You won't be able to hide me anymore

I am you and you are me

Whatever way we choose

We will always be shining

I always envied those who speak

Clearly

Eloquently

Those who can illustrate

From their first attempt

What they feel

What they want to say

Not having to replay a conversation

A million times

In your head

Faking conversations

Imagining replies

Answering contradictions

And still having the wrong words

Coming out

I try to work

while I cry

I try to smile

while I cry

I try to be there

while I cry

I collect those tears

To nourish their plants

That I am holding in my hand

The era of stills

Fake smiles

Fake relationships

We do it for the likes

We pose and force

A younger me was told

When you are older

You will be free

Free to choose

To dress

To love

To soar

As I grow

I know they were lying

Sheltering me from the truth

The older you grow

The tighter those prison bars are

I wish those times

Would be back

So I could be truly free

In the dim lighted field

I run

Around the dark corners

I hide

From all the arrows

All the questions

Targeting my soul

Am I enough ?

Will I ever understand ?

Do I belong ?

A monster is growing

That I can't keep at bay

It keeps breaking doors

As it invites me to play

At the end I know

I won't be able to keep it away

I try with all my might to stall

But the last door is about to fall

Is it the end

Will I have to bend

I refuse to be a victim

With my last breath

I will fight this dictum

Beauty is relative

I find beauty in the most mundane

In the fluttering wind

In a gentle touch

I don't search for beauty in the eyes

Not anymore

Eyes are the windows to our own

Damaged souls

It shows what we want to show

Beauty appears in actions

Not in words

In acceptance

In unsolicited guidance

In a loving embrace

I am not that shallow anymore

To look for beauty that will fade

for beauty that hides the most vicious souls

It's hard to say goodbye

To try to forget

To lock your memories away

Behind closed doors

They are never really gone

Just hidden away

It takes time and strength

To really say goodbye

To accept that someone

Will never be here again

Someone has left forever

Yet you still see them

Everyday

In your mind

In your good and bad memories

A version of them

Shaped by you

Still lives

Deeply rooted in your mind

Sometimes it's okay

To be alone

To shelter yourself

To give yourself time

To cry

To heal

To trace your scars

To have the courage

To wear them proudly

To give your soul

A chance to heal

To give your mind

An opportunity to handle

All the conflicting feelings

You are feeling

Be in that moment for as long as you need

The feeling of small butterflies

Fluttering in your stomach

As you count the seconds that pass

For you to send a reply

Asking yourself is it okay now

Will I seem too eager

If I respond now

Should I wait a little

Holding your excitement inside

Hiding behind a screen

Replying with rigid letters

That do not show how you really feel

Yet in your mind you are a little bit happy

That someone remembered you

You are protecting yourself

Building walls to shelter your heart

Giving the reigns to your mind

Just for a little time

To make sure you are on a right path

I exist

In a large universe

In a humongous galaxy

Filled with planets

And stars

I am but a small gear

Part of the big machine

In the grand scheme

But I am important

I can stop the machine

I am life

In its simplest form

When I hear the sound of rain

Pouring out

On the ground

I envy those who hear music

Feel free

I think about those who will have

To work

To clean

The dirty clothes

The muddy streets

Those who will drive their cars

Across danger

And I hope they return safely

My perspective is skewed

I stopped enjoying life a long time ago

Never ending

All will end

Someday

But we don't prepare

We just try to enjoy

Be in a moment

But it passes

And we reminiscence

And keep adding memories to moments

Making them unreal

Unrealistic

Tell stories

Miracles

About moments that has long passed

Trying to relive fiction

Mixed with a hint of truth

A paradox

A paradox I am

Alone I want to be

But I am scared

Of the uninvited guests

Looming over my soul

So I run

To other circles

To other people

Trying to protect myself

From the loud voices

In my mind

Barricading myself in circles

I know will hurt me

But the external arrows

Always hurt less

I try and pretend

That the end

Is not near

The true path will appear

The night is changing

To light

Everything becomes clear

My dark passenger is still here

I still have my fear

But for only a moment

I will persevere

I will cheer

I will hold a spear

Made from my own tears

To ward off all that is insincere

Protect myself from an old enemy

That I have been pretending not to see

Every night when I sleep

I dream of a better life

My belly swells with hope

I sleep with a never dying wish

That in the morning I will be able

To hold a new life

A new perspective towards the living

But every day I wake up bleeding

Crying from the loss

And I wonder

In the day

Maneuvering around the unknown

Lost

Fighting to protect myself

From the drawn knives

Waiting for the night

So I can hope again

We were all born

A white sheet

Free and unhinged

Without shackles

That hinder our souls

And then things are written

In our sheets

Things we can't yet understand

Things that shape us unwillingly

Shape our future

Taint our souls with color

Depending on who writes in them

Who scrambles

Who writes with love

Who writes with hate

And then we are left with

Tainted souls

Trying to wander this world

Searching for a way to erase

Delete what was written

Each day I wake up

I don't recognize the person I see

In the mirror

A changing growing body surprises me

A body that protects me

From the battles of the night

I wake up

Wondering how I got these

Thankful for a body

That tries to protect my feeble mind

Until I'm ready

I wish I could know my true feelings

I wish I could share my burdens

Together we might stand a chance

Against the darkness

I think I am ready to be here for you

I poured my love

Indiscriminately

To all

Without a limit

Until I couldn't find

Love for myself

I long for the moment

The eternal moment

When I am no longer

Burdened

By the darkness

Haunting my soul

Free from desire

Like a cocoon birthing a butterfly

I wish to be born anew

A conflicting heart

Sometimes I am a particle of sand

Drifting with the wind

With no purpose

Weak without choices

With no place to settle

No place to call home

Other times

I am a sun

With a destined purpose

A perfect path

I shine upon all things

Spread my light through

The darkest places

Helping others fight the demons

I am here for I know

There are others who depend on me

Need me to be here

They taught me that love is

Eternal

Love is perfect

Unconditional

Subliminally preparing me

For failure

Love is imperfection impersonated

Love is not eternal

It goes and comes

Sometimes it is as strong as a bond between

Atoms

Sometimes it is as feeble as a tree leaf

Coursing through the wind

Love is different to each and everyone

A word that can have many meanings as the

Number of people inhabiting this earth

I thought the more I grew

The more I will understand

Yet I've never felt

More ignorant

I spent eternities

Living in my own shadows

Trying to mend my broken heart

Weaving my broken pieces together

As I look in the mirror

Tracing the scars

I feel sorry

For myself

At the end I am the one

Left

Collecting the broken pieces

I am the one who has to

Look at all those scars

Comfort myself

To say it loudly until I believe

That it was not my fault

When I see the stars

Lighting the night

White dots scrambled

On a dark sheet

I play a game

And see how many combinations

I can create

Infinite amount of paintings

I can create

A beating heart

A crying soul

The sky is a reflection of my inner

Mind

My empty canvas

A true imperfect beauty

I am sending love

To all those who

Are fighting

Invisible battles

Struggling against

Hidden enemies

Each day

Second by second

Just to stay alive

I heard your voice today

In my dream

I panicked

Beathed heavily

I looked into my sister's eyes

Gesturing to her

Is it him

A nodding head made my heart sink into my
knees

Thought about where to hide

In the kitchen

Should I crawl

Get into the deep freezer

At the moment

I knew I was dreaming

I prayed

I never prayed so hard in my life

I prayed so hard to wake up

So I won't see you

And I woke up crying

Sad

That after all this time

You still have a hold on me

Even in my dreams

The future scares me

More than anything

Will is still be alone

Will I find my one

Will I be happy

Endless questions just

Pop up in my mind

Like daggers

Leaving unhealing scars

On my heart

I stay awake

Overthinking

And when I sleep

I dream

Of the scary future

I fear

As I grow

I am losing a lot of things

That I thought were important

To me

But nothing hits more than losing

The ability to love

Or hate

I became a neutral being

Pursuing life

With no goal

No purpose

Just existing for the sake of existing

You remind me of home

All the broken things

I had to run from

Yet I longed for

I berate myself

For being weak

Longing for a touch

A place

I know will eventually hurt me

Along this road

Alone

I walk

The sun is shining

The voices of people

Laughter surrounds me

Yet all I see is darkness

Are they laughing at me

Do they see my true self

At the end

I surrender and relinquish my desire to know

And force a smile

Upon my face

To keep them away

Keep their prying eyes

From what I want to protect

The screams of the living

Haunt me

They play on repeat

In my mind

Reminding me of all

The suffering in this world

That I can't do nothing about

A lot of pieces

I lost

On this arduous journey

And I wonder

Are these lost pieces

A part of me

That I will never be able

To get back

Or were they

A necessary step

Of my evolution

Like a butterfly

Emerging from

A cocoon

My life is a painting

With only one color

My blood

Different shades of the same color

My life is monotone

The same pessimistic view

But with different degrees of red

Oblivious

I am oblivious

That is what they get

From my blank stare

Are you here?

They ask

They don't know

They can't know

That I care too much

I observe

Their eye twitches

Their quivering lips

The tone of their voice

And my mind

Spirals

Into a vortex

Without an end

And I am scared they will know

So I just stare

Trying so hard to control

The minute muscles on my face

Threating them not to move

I practice in the mirror

To perfect my emotionless face

Threats, tears and breaking glass

In a house full of mines

I was born

Navigating my way in a war zone

Any wrong move and you will

Feel the pain

The mines changed arbitrarily

Every time I thought I knew the pattern

I was shocked

That there are new mines

Unexplainable booby traps

And as a child it was instilled in me

The safest place is to be by myself

Alone

- My childhood was shaped by the whims of a severely sick man

My dark passenger

Running away I thought

I would escape

But a passenger latched into me

Like a vampire

Sucking my life bit by bit

Like a poison

Poisoning me softly

But never killing me

Just leaving me with enough hope

So I could give it more power over me

I introjected it into my personality

Each decision I took

Was influenced by it

I ran away

Not realizing that all along

It was in me

It was fed by me

It was given life by

Decrepit

I wander alone

In my decrepit castle

Trying to mend the cracks

The falling ceiling

The shaky columns

The cracked mirrors

Showing me my shattered souls

Different variations of me

Echoing my cracked heart

I am puzzled

If I went back in time

Would my choices have been different

Or would I still make the same mistakes

So I could arrive at the current decrepit me

Cracks

Every time I start new

I anticipate the blow

I overwhelm my mind

With the anticipation

That I will fail

That life is working against me

And I collect cracks

Crack upon crack

Weighing my heart

Until I can't continue anymore

And I look for a place to run away

Deceiving myself

That if I start new

I will erase my past cracks

And the cycle repeats

Chaos

Underneath all the chaos

You see

Is a defeated soul

Waiting to be healed

A soul fractured

into millions of pieces

Spread across universes

Trying to complete the many

Troubled souls of the world

Yet denied the same help to herself

I promise if you tried

She would accept the help

From you and only you

For you have seen what is hidden

underneath

Through the words

I express myself

Write what I can't say

What I am afraid to say

Pray to be heard

Have a voice

Even if only I can read

What they see is a smile plastered

On my face

I wish I was like you

In my mind

I am swallowing my scream

Reverberating inside me

Jumbling my organs

Beating my mind with a bat

Trying to numb it

So I won't feel as much as I do

Burning my nerve endings

While my inner voice

Shrieks at people

Please stop looking into my smile

And stare at me eyes

It will show you the truth

They were searching for fireworks

The drama

Some action, they said

that was not the love I wanted

neither needed

What I offered was something profound

Love is calm and deep

A constant faith

Quiet and lasting

A warm hug after a long day

Not a loud shout at every corner

I couldn't continue caring for the
unpredictable

The ups and downs of a twisted mind

So I made a choice for myself

My wellbeing

My mental health

And I left

I bathe myself

In a river of compassion

Try to wash away

My past mistakes

So I can at least

Have the courage

To look at myself

Eye to eye

And say

I have tried

They taught me to always look

For the eyes

Observe it well

Cause it never lies

And I spent ages looking

And the only thing I learned

Just like everyone else

The eyes can lie too

We learn to hide it

Bury our truths

Behind doors of encryptions

With different meanings showing

Depending on different situations

Training on how to obscure

Our feelings because we are scared

That someone would use them

Against us

Against the wizards of time

I will prevail

I will set my story in stones

They won't be able to erase

All my scars, my demons

Will be ingrained

Will be my witnesses

On the cruel world

I had to endure

Be free like a bird

Fly high in the sky

Yet we don't ask

Is the bird free

Uncertain worried

Always searching for my next meal

Afraid

Floating endlessly

Flying against extreme winds

I'd rather be a turtle

Strong, safe and protected

By my own shell of strength

I could survive on so little

Walk slowly but certain of my steps

Taking my own time

To process my life

Does it hurt ?

They keep reminding me

Yeah it hurts

I can't seem to forget

I ran and ran away

Time after time

As fast as I could

But it keeps coming after me

Living in my shadow

Does it hurt ?

Do you really want to know ?

Like a million knives ripping through

my heart

Yeah it hurts

I want to scream through this void

Let them feel my pain

but why let others

Walk in my shoes

This pain is mine alone

Bearing it is the sin I have

To endure

I am fighting with all my might

To prove them wrong

But I know deep inside

That my inevitable defeat

I can't prolong

In a voice I trained so well

I take a stand and yell

With a voice so deep and loud

I try to make myself proud

I look in the mirror

with a little bit of pride

With a lowered voice and a lowered gaze

I say at least I have tried

We are born

Free

Unshackled

to soar in the sky

But we are forced

To carry the mountains

That were supposed

To be climbed

Forgiveness

You try to be free

Of the hatred

That has grown so deep

In your heart

Travelling through your veins

To every inch of your weak body

So you try and forgive

As hard as you can

And for just a little bit of time

You forget the hatred

But then you hear

The screams

Of your scars

Reminding you of the pain

Telling you that they are not

Worthy

Of your forgiveness

I was sick of waiting

I sharpened my sword

I won't wait for them to find me

I will fight my demons

And go out

Into the wilderness

Filled with hatred

Which I will use

As my fuel

To lit the fire

Of the furnace

That will strengthen my sword

They didn't see it coming

When I jumped

Into the middle of the fire

They are so young

They pitied

They must have been sick

They judged

Little they know

That I used the fire

To temper my soul

That with my own free will

And with sound mind

I chose to dive

Into the danger

So that I can be me

Through the desert

I wander

Searching for what can

Quench the needs of my heart

Search for my damaged soul

That has lost its way

Following the footsteps of those

Who wandered before

I see glimpses of my past self

Smell my fear through the air

Small proofs

That give me hope

That I still exist

That I am still out there

Trying

At the dusk of dawn

We met

No exchange of names

Address or any information

That might provide danger

To anonymity

We agreed

For the first time

I felt free

Without mountains on my back

I unloaded

All my demons

I shared the weight and horror

That I have held on for so long

Or so I thought

As for every demon I shared

A new one appeared

Unknown undefined

Demons I couldn't control

Demons I couldn't bury deep

Demons I couldn't ignore

And I realized the mistake I made

I exchanged the demons I grew accustomed to

With new kinds of demons

That are harder to please

Harder to put to sleep

And with new mountains on my back

I walked away

They tend to forget

All you have done for them

All the tears and the sweat

You used to help them grow

From tiny seeds

To giant trees

After they used your shade

To hide from the predators

They now shoo you away

They dare to accuse you

Of stealing their sun

Preventing them from glowing

That you want them

To always be in your shade

Yet what I only wanted was

To shield them from harm

They suck your nutrients dry

And then leave

Without a goodbye

Leaving you with a sense of failure

That you have not done enough

That you should have shed more tears

More sweat

My castle

In my castle of memories

I fantasize

About broken memories

That play on repeat on my mind

Everchanging

Depending on my mood

Sometimes I am happy

As a child eating ice cream

Other times I am sorrowful

As an old weak tree

Regretting every decision

I ever made

Yet I always escape

To my castle

So I can dream

And live a life I don't have the courage

To live

Envy

In these roads we are travelling

There are those who care

Who light the darkness

They were once lost

So they help guide the disoriented

While others are scared

That someone will go further than they have

So they wreck havoc

Destroy lamps

Bury street signs

Burn maps

And invent fake excuses

Just so they remain ahead

They don't know life is complicated

With many roads

With different destinations

At the end they will be left alone

For every hand that destroys

A thousand guides

Two faced

I have learned from my past

Mistakes

I smile and nod

Pretend to ponder

And agree

Just leave them believing

That you still believe them

Believe their deceiving thorns

Wrapped around shiny flowers

I smile and nod

Accept their gift

And just leave it there

I won't let their thorns penetrate me

Not again

I will listen with deaf ears

I will see with blind eyes

And if they try harder

I will gift them their thorns back

Without any wrapping

My honest thorns

Relinquished

You are standing alone

Nude

No possessions

Friends have left you

Loved ones relinquished you

The roads have separated you

Walls built around you

You can hear them

Yet they are so far away

You think if you wait for them

They will come back to you

Telling you how good a friend you were

But they have long abandoned you

Yet you can't let go of your fantasies

Silently

I scream with an ear-piercing voice

Yet no voice comes out

I cry with shrieking noise

Yet no one hears

Silently I suffer

Waiting for someone

Who will never come

Someone who has left

With my heart in his hand

I am sitting on the docks

For a train that has no arrival time

Just my unfounded hope

That someday they will come for me

And I silently wait

When did it happen to me

When saying their name

Feels like a crime

Against my mental health

I thought I had moved on

By getting away

But I was only running

Towards my cage

I thought I was free

From their hold on me

But I was only digging

My own grave

A little bit deeper

With every step

Free time is a thing I fear

Making myself busy

With frivolous matters

So that my brain stops working

For a little bit of time

To get a couple of minutes

To take my breath

Get prepared

For when

I reminisce

My scars open again

All those memories

I have of you

Constantly remind me

Of all the things I have lost

I am scared to commit again

For I fear the hold that your memories

Have on me

I search for your smile

On every new face I see

I am not scared to be lonely

A life alone is what I am used to

What truly terrifies me is all those memories

That do not die

The emptiness consumes me

Threatening

To erase me from existence

Turning me into a machine

I cannot ignore

The hole that they left

I am trying

To mend it

With new things

But when they left

They took a part of me

That I can't replace

I visit all the place we have been to

Thinking that I might find

The missing piece

To fill the void inside me

But all I that I feel

Is the emptiness getting stronger

Feeding on my loneliness

It hurts

Thinking that you are with someone

Else

And I am alone

Thinking about our time

Together

I hope you are happy

But it hurts

That you moved on

Yet I can't

What I loved has become a memory

In my mind

A perfect being created

With no flaws

That I reminisce about

While you are human

With imperfections

That I choose to ignore

While telling myself

It was my fault

That you left

That's why

It still hurts

A stranger

I lost a lot that day

I still remember it as if it was

Yesterday

You kept turning

You couldn't sleep

It wasn't you

And I had to ask

The dreaded question

A question I was running from

A question deep in my heart

I knew the answer to

What's wrong ?

And I could see the answer

In your eyes

Before hearing it

I wanted to scream

Why ?

Did I wrong you in any way ?

I wanted to cry

I wished I could cry

But your answer built a barrier

Between us

You were sitting right in front of me

But I felt you were miles away

I was a proud person

I wouldn't cry in front of a stranger

I held it in

And you became someone

I couldn't open up to anymore

A stranger

Every place the wind carries me is home

I am a wanderer

I float on water

I ski on land

Yet a part of nature

I aspire to be

A being with so much love

To give

That I wish mother nature

Would accept me into its bosoms

Feed me with the immortality nectar

Help me plant roots

So I can become immovable

Find a place to finally call home

I am moving in circles

Round and round

I dance

To the beat of my own sorrow

Stationary like a statue

I am deceiving myself

I am running in place

Tired without going anywhere

Lifeless without a goal

An end to a life

I didn't choose to be born into

Orphan

I feel like a discarded root

Cut from an old tree

Unwanted

And left to rot

A brick on the side of the road

Drifting from place to place

With no goal

Based on the whims of strangers

I keep running in circles

Around the same thought

Again and again

Day after day

Year after year

Am I enough?

After a success I cower

And I wonder

Do I deserve it ?

And after each failure

A thought is born inside my womb

That I was the reason

Abortion was the solution

I should just shut up and smile

And in circles I dance

Waiting for the moment I get tired

So I can dose off for a bit

I am scared

Of the loneliness

Scared of how much I love it

Being embraced by it

Bathed in the glory of my own sun

The safety of my own embrace

Will this be the ultimate end

Being closed off in my on cage

The only window is up

Where I can see the sun shining

Waiting for it to rise

instead of chasing it through the wilderness

Will this cement surrounding me shield me

From the uncertainties of change

Sometimes I climb so I can observe

A little better

And I wonder

What would happen

If I go all the way up

Never look back

And chase the sun

Sometimes I forget

A memory

And I wonder

Did I block this part of me

Locked it and threw away the key

To help my fragile mind

Cope with reality

Time

Do I have the time ?

To cry every night

To die everyday

To be a walking corpse

To be a sheep among the herd

Too scared to branch out

I am tired of just existing for the sake of

Existing

I am not pretty

I say to myself

As I look in the mirror

I see tears falling down

Silently

as if afraid

To confirm the truth

That I won't be as pretty as them

That my nose won't be as small theirs

That no matter how much makeup I plaster on my face

I won't have their skin tone

I know I am unique in my own way

Accepted that I will always be

A lone wolf

Destined to be alone

I just wish to have company sometimes

I've tried to be with you

In the darkness of the night

I held my pillow

Close to my chest

Dreaming

Imagining

It was you I was embracing

But the only true thing

I woke up to

Were my wet sheets

From all the tears

I've shed

I have done all I can

But this fear

Won't leave me alone

Like a shadow

Sucking my life away

Eating me inside out

Until nothing is left

Only an empty shell

remains

Filled to the brim

With my own fears

I often find myself

Wondering

Whether people would like me

If they could see my soul

If physical appearance was not

What we judge people for

Will people come and talk to me

Will they be my friends

Is my soul as beautiful as I think it is

Or am I just making excuses for my own

Cowardice

My inability to cut off what hurts me

My constant hunger for approval

For all the wrong reasons

From all the wrong people

worrying

I live in a constant state of worry

About tomorrow

Next week

About the uncertainties of the future

Robbed little by little

Of moments I should have lived

Moments I should have experienced

Moments of joy

But instead

Here I am

Dwelling on imaginary things

That might or might not happen

Leaving me in a constant state of disarray

How do I find the person in my dreams

The one I shared the sunsets

and the shooting stars with

The person whose hugs would

Erase all my pain away

The person whose arm would

Breath life into me

Tell me its okay it'll get better

Maybe not today

But the future is uncertain

And I'll be here for you

Will I ever find them

I am walking around

With a fire burning my head

A fire only I can see

Eating me

From the inside

and I have to hold my anger

And screams inside

As I can't prove a pain

Only I can see

Surrender

My life is a mess

I fight battles that I don't need to

I stretch myself thin

And then complain

Sometimes the winning choice

Is to surrender

Not the fight

But the choice to fight

- Not all battles are worth fighting

Abandonment

I tend to hoard

All the things I bought or were gifted to me

Are stored

And loved

Even when they stop functioning

They are still loved nonetheless

I guess I am overcompensating

Because I do not want to be left alone

-I fear abandonment

Running away

I was running

And I am still running away

From their staring accusing eyes

When will I stop

Running away

When will I stop

Being afraid

Of things I can not control

I have to take a stand

That is what the voice in my mind

Is telling me

In my bed at night

But when the sun comes it disappears

Sometimes I try and stay up

So the voice stays with me

But no matter what I do

I fail

And my courageous inner voice vanishes

Without trace

Dark spots

In my memories

There are many dark spots

Events that I have blocked

Moments that have been robbed

From me

Time that I will not get back

I want to remember

To get stronger

To learn from my past

But I keep falling back

Into the same mistakes

And for a while I remember

But my feeble mind tries hard

To protect me

And a new dark spot is formed

People jump into my pool of mystery

Intrigued by the peaceful surface

Wondering about this enigmatic person

They meet

They are intrigued by the eternal smile

Plastered on my face

My willingness to listen

To offer help

Without expectations

But then they find that the pool

Is an ocean full of mysteries

they can not fathom

Filled with waves and whirlwinds

And they run away

People ask me

Why do you reply so fast

And I reply

If my phone is in my hand

Why would I not ?

And in my mind

I think that they must be doing this to me

If they are telling me to do this to others

Frustrated

I want an explanation

No I need an explanation

Why things won't work for me

Every new road

Ends with a dead end

Every new relationship

Ends with a heart break

I try to feel hopeful

Smile and move on

Maybe I am the disease

That need to be cured

But I can't seem to understand

The medicine I need

Instant relief

In a world plagued with speed

I search for the slowness of snails

to be able to take my time

To learn

And develop

To be able to be there for myself

To Live in the moment

I will take it slow

Search for the uniquely mundane

In a place filled with shining stars

I look for those with hidden light

As stars with shiniest and brightest light

Are the fastest to dim and wither

Abd contrary to those who have been hurt
before

Hurt stars know how to hide their light

Like beacons on the sea

They choose who deserves to see their

True self

Choices

Life is mainly composed of choices

Whether to Stay on land

Safely

Or take a risk

And jump into the sea

Where the storm looms

And danger is abundant as water droplets

Yet it is the same for me

As safety is deceptive

When your demons are your worst enemy

When you are the only one you can depend

On

When you are the only one you can trust

It doesn't matter land or sea

My demons will always be with me

A garden

My garden is full of memories

Blooming out of the ground

many are red

As if my blood was used to feed them

many are black

As the night

With thorns hurting my skin

Few are multi colored

Surrounded by black and red

Weak and feeble

As I try to water them

The reds and the blacks

Block my pathway

Preventing me from getting near

I try and fight for a moment or two

Many times I fail

But sometimes I succeed

And my tears of joy water my unique flowers

Exquisite

In the name of beauty

I suffer

I starve

Just so I can hear those poisonous words

You are beautiful

So I can feel validated

Externally at least

I hate the way I require others' opinion

On things that affect me and only me

What if they think I am ugly

Or chubby

The only opinion that matters is mine and
mine alone

Phoenix

Sometimes I think about burning it all

The memories that brought us together

The history we shared

And rise from their ashes

Anew like a phoenix

But then I remember that those lessons

Taught me a lot

Those lessons made me who I am today

Every scar and every tear

Define me

And I won't change that for the world

Plink

I used to hate the sound of water droplets

In the kitchen sink

Drip after drip

Annoying as a child's screams on an air plane

Consistent

No matter what I use to fix it

It does not matter

The next day at night

The sound would appear again

Like a human filled with emotions

Who has been hurt so many times

That they can't share no more

But every once in a while when the tank is full

then their emotions seep

And drip for a while

until they can hold it in again

They can't control the time nor the quantity

And they seem unaware of it while it's happening

And when they realize it

They blame themselves for their relapse of judgement

Leaving me stranded on an empty island

I used to share

Tell you everything I know

You knew all my highs and lows

Ups and downs

You were there

You were the only one who I confided to

What I really wanted to become

But not only you let me go

You plastered my stories on the walls

My deepest secrets

For everyone to see

To know

All my fears and failures

You left me stranded

In an open sea

Surrounded by danger

And you left

- I couldn't share anything with anyone again

My sour companion

I wish it was like fashion

Ephemeral

But instead it's long lasting

Eternal

Haunting me day and night

Every where I go

It's shrouding my sight

Shaping my vision

Interfering in every decision

I make

Sometimes it is caring and sweet

Promising me a treat

But it's a pretense

To leave me without defense

Robing me of my common sense

The fire raging inside me

I stare at the fire

Watching it grow larger

Scarier

And hotter

Threating to engulf me

As I am feeding it

Wishing it would fizzle

- contradiction

through the desert

I wander and wonder

Against the razor-sharp winds

Through the droughts

Accompanied by the loneliness

And the sounds of my beating heart

Looking for medicine

To heal my plagued soul

Following old traces of those who came
before me

Deducing from the increasing distance
between those traces

That the end is near

But I can't help it

I am starting to lose hope

That my soul won't like the medicine I will find

But I know it will be the medicine I need

Not what I want

Untethered

I wish I was free

Like the dizziness you feel

The moment you suddenly stand

And you feel momentarily

That you are untethered from the world

You forget everything

All the luggage you have been

dragging behind your back

You feel weightless

As if you could fly

And as suddenly as it comes

It goes

And the euphoric moment disappears

And I am back into the real world

The doubt

The wind whispers quietly in my ear

Constantly

Casting doubt in my heart

Telling me not to run

That what is here is better than what is
unknown

Better than what is undefined

The constant nagging muddles my mind

With conflicting thoughts

Preventing me from making a decision

Making me ponder if this was what it really
wants

Making me stand on the edge

Between land and water

Never taking a step in either direction

Worshipping a false idol

I am jealous

Of the me I created

In my mind

The perfect happy version of me

The one who smiles ear to ear

Extends a helping hand to all those in need

But then I grew up

And my perfect image turned into burdens

And expectations from others

I needed to be perfect for my younger self

To be happy

I searched for validation in how others looked
at me

- I guess what I really wanted is to be loved

Suns by the millions

Up in the sky

There exists

A million suns

Shining above us

Giving birth to new worlds

Filled with new life

Yet here I am wishing

I was never born

Scared

I was standing alone

Like a wet towel

Scared of the unknown

Waiting to go dry

To be free again

Yet every time I am close to being wet free

I jump back into the water

Frightened that I'll have to face others again

Creating an excuse to keep me safe

In my isolation

Surrounded by what I find familiar

The aware skeptic

It is not healthy

How I doubt each kind gesture directed
towards me

I am aware of my short comings

But I can't stop wondering

Why would anyone do a good deed for me

Me who were bitten so many times

What do they need from me

And it became a little habit of mine

To never accept help

And never ask for it

Find someone to talk to

how easy is it for them to say

Just go to therapy

It will help

How do they expect me to trust someone

Lay down all my vulnerabilities

And be naked in front of them

And ask for help

My mind can't fathom the possibility

Of being indebted to others

A soul heading to no where

They said shed your fears

Chase away your demons

Be free of what they said you are

And now I don't know what defines me
anymore

What am I ?

I don't have a goal nor a dream

I am just wandering aimlessly blindly

hoping to find the route

At least when they said I was fat

I told myself I could go to the gym

And when they said I am not pretty enough

I started to wear more make up

Now I blocked their words

I started to accept myself slowly

But what to do now

I hope I can figure it out

Before I am drawn back to my old familiar
ways

The smell of butter

Is a ticket to older times

Like riding a time machine

Into the past

When I was happy

When the small pleasures made me content

When the smell of butter

Could make my saliva drool in anticipation

Of homemade cookies

It reminds me of family

Where my ultimate desire

Was to finish homework early

So that I can watch my favorite show

It was a smell of simpler times

Delirious

We walk in this world

Delirious

Unaware of our true desires

Like sheep in a herd

Guided by false prophets

That we are bombarded with

Day and night

How to live

How to speak

How to relieve yourself

As if they monopolized life

That their way is the only way

It is the true way

And others don't have your best interest

We became so intoxicated in being told how
to live

That we have no natural desires anymore

Our life is dictated by others